The Common Good

The Catholic Church's Social Teaching

Kevin Mayhew

First published in 1997 by
KEVIN MAYHEW LTD
Rattlesden
Bury St Edmunds
Suffolk IP30 0SZ

The Common Good © 1996 The Bishops'
Conference of England and Wales.
This abridged edition and questions
© 1997 Kevin Mayhew Ltd.

All rights reserved. No part of this publication may be
reproduced, stored in a retrieval system, or transmitted,
in any form or by any means, electronic, mechanical,
photocopying, recording or otherwise, without the
prior written permission of the publisher.

0 1 2 3 4 5 6 7 8 9

ISBN 0 86209 944 7
Catalogue No 1500088

Front cover design by Graham Johnstone

Compiled and edited by Helen Wynne
Typesetting by Louise Hill
Printed and bound in Great Britain

Contents

Preface by Cardinal Basil Hume,
Archbishop of Westminster   4

PART I
Christian Citizens in Modern Britain   7

PART II
Application to Contemporary Questions   21

Preface by Cardinal Basil Hume
Archbishop of Westminster

It is the task of bishops of the Church to preach and teach the Gospel; to point people in the direction of Christ. Religion is never just a private affair. Discipleship involves seeking God in this world, as well as preparing to meet him in the next. The Gospel imperative to love our neighbour entails not only that we should help those in need, but also address the causes of destitution and poverty.

Over the past year the bishops of England and Wales have been considering some of these issues with a view to presenting them to the Catholic community as a fundamental part of the teaching of the Church. This document is the result.

The foundation of this teaching is the dignity of the human person. Each of us is made in the image and likeness of God. Society must therefore first of all respect and protect human life itself – at all its stages from conception to its natural end. This is the bedrock of our civilisation.

Our human dignity also consists in our being made free by God. Society should therefore respect human freedom by enabling men and women to assume responsibility for their own lives, and encouraging them to co-operate with each other to pursue the common good.

The Church has the right and the duty to advocate a social order in which the human dignity of all is fostered, and to protest when it is in any way threatened. Every public policy should be judged by the effect it has on human dignity and the common good.

The Church does not present a political programme, still less a party political one. Its teaching provides a set of consistent and complementary principles, values and goals. There will be scope for debate about how best to achieve these.

The Church's social teaching places the political within the larger context of humanity's relationship with God. Social and political action is important, but realising our full human dignity as children of God also requires each of us to undertake an inner spiritual journey. The future of humanity does not depend on political reform, social revolution or scientific advance. Something else is needed. It starts with a true conversion of mind and heart.

CARDINAL BASIL HUME
ARCHBISHOP OF WESTMINSTER
PRESIDENT OF THE BISHOPS'
CONFERENCE OF ENGLAND AND WALES

PART I

CHRISTIAN CITIZENS IN MODERN BRITAIN

Introduction

The document, *The Common Good*, offered by the Bishops of England and Wales as a contribution to the deepening of public debate in this pre-election period, comes in a long tradition of Catholic Social Teaching throughout the ages. It has seen particular development in the last one hundred years through the social encyclicals of successive Popes, up to and including the considerable contribution of the present Pontiff. It is hoped that the timing of this document will enable Catholics and others to reflect on their choices in the light of the Church's teaching and the specific problems of our society today and to act responsibly for the common good.

In speaking at this time, the Bishops are not 'playing politics', but rather exercising what influence they have and sharing their wisdom and experience on behalf of the powerless.

The Church's heritage of wisdom and revelation is available for all. But it is a Church which listens as well as teaches, one which welcomes dialogue.

The Church's right to be heard

Throughout the centuries of Christianity, the Church has laboured for the alleviation of poverty of all kinds in these islands. Its contribution still, in investment of money and people, is enormous. It has long experience of collaboration with State and professional bodies, as well as first-hand knowledge of the harsh realities of poverty.

A DISTINCTIVE VISION

In working for the desperately poor, and in its untiring efforts to develop and maintain a just social order, the Church brings to the task a distinctive moral and spiritual vision. This vision is based on the fundamental truth that the human person is made in the image of God and is the reflection of God among us. This vision colours everything the Church does and teaches. Because of it we can say that

- to serve our neighbour, especially when he or she is poor, is a privilege and a duty, because it is Christ that we are serving in them.

The dignity of the human person comes from the fact that he or she is created in the image of God, and not from any human accomplishments, economic status, gender or race.

It is not only the Church which must recognise human dignity; all human institutions must do so as well.

What aspects of human life convince me that human beings are more than a bundle of chromosomes?

What does 'image of God' mean?

Where does the phrase come from?

- The test of every institution or policy is whether it enhances or threatens human dignity and indeed human life itself.

> How would I rate the institutions to which I belong and which I support?
>
> Do they, perhaps, have one set of policies at home and another for the developing world?

- Policies which treat people as mere economic units, or which oblige people to live on welfare, do not respect the dignity of the human person.

> Could I apply this test to the manifestos I shall be hearing over the next few months?

Since we are all made in the likeness of God, then we are all brothers and sisters, rich and poor alike.

- To help our brother or sister is a duty, not a burden.

understand the reality and work to remove the evil structures.

One of the structures which enhances the development of persons is the family, the smallest unit of community, the basic cell of society. The human race itself can be described as a 'community of communities', existing at international, national, regional and local level.

- A well-constructed society will be one that gives priority to the integrity, stability and health of family life.

- No law should be passed with possible social consequences without first considering what effect it would have on family life and especially on children.

Can I name three structures/laws which enhance the development of children in my society?

Can I name three which actively hinder this development?

Catholic Social Teaching
Through the Years

Throughout the years the Church has studied how societies function and what principles should guide them. In the last one hundred years, as social patterns have undergone rapid change, it has intensified that study. This study forms the basis of Catholic Social Teaching.

This teaching works from a global perspective and is well informed. In recent decades it has shown a more Christ-centred, and therefore more person-centred, approach.

This teaching is aimed at the formation of conscience as a basis for action. It is for groups to decide how to apply it in particular circumstances. Some of its elements are direct applications of the moral law and are not open to debate. For example, it teaches that genocide and racial hatred are wrong.

It has, at times, reflected too closely the particular historic circumstances of the age. Subsequent teaching has tried to correct this bias.

- Catholic Social Teaching is not just to be found in Church documents. It is lived and living in people's lives.

It is desirable that the members of the Church be more involved in the formulation of its social teaching. This involvement is an application of one of the two social principles which this document especially highlights: that of *subsidiarity*.

THE SOCIAL DIMENSION OF FAITH

- In God there are three Persons united in love: Father, Son and Holy Spirit. The desire of human beings to belong to society is God-given.

It is both a reflection of the love between the Persons in God and a response to it.

> **When I see love in action all around me, how do I explain this phenomenon?**

Living in society, however, makes demands, both on individuals and on societies as a whole. This means that individuals and societies must live by moral principles if they are to be allowed to live and to develop as persons made in God's image.

- Not all of the ways in which society is structured are conducive to human development. Some actively hinder it.

The Church uses the term 'structures of sin' in this regard.

But structures of sin come from personal sin and from the concrete acts of individuals. The Church urges us to name the source of the evil, so that we can begin to

> **What images in the media come to me when I read this?**
>
> **Any songs, poems or films I know?**

This relationship extends to all people; it has global implications. This is what the document understands by *solidarity*.

Solidarity with my neighbour worldwide is about the promotion of equal rights and opportunities for all, and the condemnation of all forms of discrimination and racism. It involves the willingness to see others as another 'self', and to react towards injustice in their regard as I would if it were an injustice against myself.

> **Again, how is the principle of solidarity respected by the institutions I support, the government of my country, in my immediate family?**

• This responsibility for the welfare of the whole of society is part of my religious duties as a Catholic, and just as important as attending Church.

> **Do I keep these two in proper balance?**

Meaning of 'subsidiarity'

- Subsidiarity involves the passing of powers downwards, but also upwards. It supports a sharing of authority as close to the grass roots as good government allows.

Over the years, the Church has been critical of systems of government which proclaim economic determinism, whether capitalist or communist, whether of the right or of the left. The encyclical *Rerum Novarum* of Pope Leo XIII and other encyclicals have led the way in restating the primacy of the human over the economic and the spiritual and moral over the material.

Now that Marxist Communism is not a force, what correctives to the excesses of free-market capitalism are there in our present society?

Does the democratic process itself need checks and balances?

Fundamental features of our society

The Church's teaching now fully embraces two fundamental features of modern society about which it once had some difficulties: democracy and human rights.

- Catholic Social Teaching reminds us that democracy can never justify immoral policies.

It is 'not a self-sufficient moral system': universal suffrage is not enough. There must also be 'a system of common values' for democracy to function morally.

- We need to have an understanding of the common good if democracy is not to risk becoming a 'democratic tyranny in which the majority oppresses the minority'. Those authorities responsible for the common good also have to be democratically appointed.

What do I understand by the common good?

Can I identify leaders in our democratic society who share these values?

- The so-called 'right to choose' is a frequently misused term. We do not have a right to choose to do harm.
- Stress on rights must be coupled with an equivalent stress on duties.

That being said, individuals do have a claim on each other and on society for certain basic minimum conditions without which the value of human life is diminished or even negated. States may ignore them, but nobody can take these rights from us. They originate from our creation in the image of God. From this fundamental right to life the rest flows: decent housing, health care, freedom of speech, education, the right to raise and provide for a family.

- Every member of the community has a duty to the common good in order that the rights of others may be satisfied and their freedoms respected.

> Which rights and freedoms do I see being eroded in society today: in Britain? Elsewhere?
>
> What action can I take to prevent or slow this trend?
>
> What initiatives can I name that are working to this end?

- Catholic Social Teaching emphasises the link between spreading the Good News of the Gospel and empowering people.

> Could I explain this link clearly, if asked by an unbeliever? If not, who can I ask to help me clarify it?

The Catholic practice of 'examination of conscience' should include questioning ourselves on what we know of the Church's social teaching and how we should apply it. This would be a particularly useful exercise before a general election.

Adherence to the Church's social teaching is every bit as important as observing other aspects of the Church's moral teaching. There is a link which should not be forgotten between structural and personal sin.

Do I find this balance reflected in sermons? The Media? My personal examination of conscience?

CATHOLIC SOCIAL TEACHING
AND NATURAL LAW

Besides Scripture itself, natural law is one of the chief bases on which the Church builds its social teaching. This source is available to everyone. Medieval England drew on it for the concept of natural justice which in turn gave rise to Common Law.

Common Law was an expression of existing social consensus as to what was right and wrong. Natural law has a close relationship to Revelation. It is found implicitly too in other faiths.

The application of natural law is often controversial.

- In applying natural law, however, political judgment needs to be guided by first principles.

- Society must be organised around the common good rather than the interests of the few.

- To ignore natural law is to collaborate with the structures of sin.

What, then, is the common good?

The common good is the whole network of social conditions which enable human individuals and groups to flourish and live a fully, genuinely human life, otherwise described as 'integral human development'.

- All are responsible for all, collectively and as individuals.

How might this apply in the danger-ridden streets of modern society?

How does the parable of the Good Samaritan (Luke 10:30ff.) cast light on this dilemma?

Meaning of 'solidarity'

The determination to commit oneself to this responsibility for the common good of all is what the Bishops mean by 'solidarity'. It is not merely vague compassion or shallow distress.

At the same time, the assumption of responsibility or the giving of help must never be allowed to destroy people or absorb them. It must, wherever possible, respect people's right to an active role in deciding what is best for all. This is the sister principle of subsidiarity. The two principles must operate in tandem.

PART II

APPLICATION TO CONTEMPORARY QUESTIONS

Interpreting the Signs of the Times

The Church would be failing in moral courage if its social teaching remained at a general level in order to avoid controversy. As bishops we have a duty to discern and interpret the signs of the times.

There are trends in British society and public life today which seem to us to be contrary to Catholic teaching, as well as features of public and private morality which are commendable.

Which trends in society would I commend?

Which would I criticise?

Why?

We acknowledge the strong Christian tradition in British politics. Nonetheless we are concerned about the low esteem in which politics is held today. This is an unhealthy trend which is neither justified by the evidence nor good for democracy. The mass media is not blameless in fostering this climate of cynicism and distrust.

- Political debate in Britain badly needs remoralising and an injection of humility.

> **In what ways do I contribute to this climate of cynicism and distrust?**
>
> **How do I react to character assassination in the media?**
>
> **If I dislike it, what do I do about it?**

APPROACHING AN ELECTION

Under the British constitution, those elected to parliament are not mere delegates.

- Political allegiance therefore is not the only consideration when voting for a candidate. A general election is not a single-issue referendum. Issues may arise later which were not on the cards at election time.

- It is essential then to take into account a candidate's moral attitudes and character.

It is important to ask ourselves:

- Will this candidate be the best person to make judgments on my behalf, when other issues arise later?

- What are the candidates' policies and what is the reasoning behind them?

This consideration will discourage the making of a choice solely on the basis of one policy issue alone, even where the attitudes of a candidate on such an issue are at variance with Catholic teaching. On the other hand, the attitude of a candidate on that one issue may indicate a general philosophy or personal bias, for instance contempt for those who uphold the sacredness of human life, which Catholics will find deeply objectionable.

How well informed am I on where candidates actually stand on, say,
abortion,
the arms trade,
aid to developing countries?

How can I find out?

Could I 'examine my conscience' on my progress in this matter every week between now and the general election?

Could I attend/organise a meeting and ask candidates to share their views? Most of them will welcome a platform.

The Right to Life

In Britain today human life has been devalued; we have a 'culture of death' where consciences have been blunted and abortion is now widely regarded as a remedy for any social or personal difficulties.

- We have to raise our voices in protest against all destruction of human life in the womb.

We must resist the current tendency to use personal convenience as an acceptable basis for decision-making on other ethical issues too:
> treatment of those brain-dead or permanently unconscious;
> the elderly suffering from terminal illness;
> human embryos conceived outside the womb as part of fertility treatment.

- Medical ethics must be securely rooted in respect for human life at all its stages.

- Everything involving the use or disposal of human life, as a means to another end, must be categorically rejected.

The Catholic community must renew its efforts to awaken the conscience of the majority in these matters.

How well informed am I on Catholic teaching on these matters?

When test cases in the media are being discussed, am I prepared to stand up and be counted?

THE COMMON GOOD AND HUMAN WELFARE

The common good is a central concept in Catholic Social Teaching. It is seen as the guarantor of individual rights and the context in which conflicts of individual rights and interests can be judged.

- The common good is the responsibility of those in authority.

Every individual, however, must promote it as well as benefit from it. 'Common' here means that it extends to all sectors of the population.

- Society, then, must be run for the benefit of all its members.

It is not enough to ensure that people do not starve or lack shelter.

Ultimately there comes a point when the gap between rich and poor begins to undermine the good of all.

Jesus' warning to the rich young man about attachment to material riches applies to communities as well as to individuals.

> Could I read this Gospel story again in Luke 18:18 alone, or with a few friends, and see how it might apply today?

• The Church teaches that there is an obligation on every individual to contribute to the common good.

This is in the interests of justice and in line with the 'option for the poor'.

It is, moreover, in the interests of an orderly, prosperous and healthy society. A society which did not have regard for the common good would be unpleasant and dangerous to live in.

> What decisions do I personally make that are in line with the common good and the 'option for the poor' in our society?

Market forces

While recognising the positive value of business, the market, private property and free human creativity in the economic sector, the Church points out that

- market forces are not always in line with the common good.

The poor in our society are often excluded from having a voice in policy making and so have no protection from the adverse consequences of market forces. They have little freedom of choice.

- The common good requires of each citizen to ensure that nobody is marginalised in this way, that nobody feels that they do not count in society.

Morality in the market place

Unlimited free-market capitalism is entirely driven by market forces. This theory presupposes that the common good will take care of itself.

To say that this will invariably happen, or to say that in promoting my own gain I am automatically promoting the good of society, is manifestly not true.

- Left to themselves, market forces are just as likely to lead to evil results as to good ones.

The end result of market forces must, then, be scrutinised, in the name of social justice, human rights, and the common good.

Which economic situations or decisions, dictated by market forces, do I not approve of? Why?

This is not to deny that market forces, regulated in the interests of the common good, can be an efficient way of matching resources to need and of encouraging the creation of wealth for the alleviation of need.

Wider consumer choice enables individuals to exercise freedom and to express their views. Competition can encourage creativity. The principles of subsidiarity and solidarity can be served.

However, the Church reminds us that

- an economic method is not a world view or an ideology to live one's life by.

An economic creed that encourages self-interest as a road to the greater good of society is likely to find itself encouraging individual selfishness, for the sake of the economy.

The effects of such an ethos on public and private morality soon become evident. Society cannot have its cake and eat it.

Christianity, on the other hand, places service of others above service of self.

There is a conflict of ethos here.

People need more encouragement to be unselfish than to be selfish. It is not difficult to imagine which message will be more influential. A wealthy society, however, if it is a greedy society, is not a good society. This is why the Church has been cautious about free market economics for more than a hundred years.

Where do I find this conflict of ethos evident in my society today?

AN OPTION AGAINST THE POOR?

The Bishops feel that the time is ripe to re-emphasise the concept of the common good.

DUTIES OF PUBLIC AUTHORITIES

Those in public authority have a duty to judge between the conflicting demands of a market economy and those of the common good. Using the common good as the criterion, they must weigh up which economic activities can be left to market forces and which require provision in part or in full by the State.

They must be alert and ensure that deficiencies in essential social provision such as health and education are quickly put right, rather than allowing institutions to go under owing to market pressures, harming those who rely on them.

What is the track-record in this regard of the political party I support?

There are some professions where the traditional motives of vocation and dedication to others, or to the public good, have been damaged by the search for profit. The social services and the service of government come particularly to mind.

- The search for profit must not be allowed to override all other moral considerations.

> **If I am a shareholder, however small, in any company I have a voice. How do I use it?**
>
> **As a customer, I can vote with my feet. How much do I know about the policies of, say, my local supermarket chain?**
>
> **What do I know of their record in the developing world?**
>
> **Their staff relations policy?**

Advertising plays a role in creating a society where the satisfaction of real or artificial needs takes priority over all else.

- The individual begins to have value only as a consumer, a possessor of wealth and a purchaser of goods. This is contrary to the Gospel and to any rational idea of what a human being really is. It gravely disadvantages those who do not have wealth to spend.

In a competition-driven market, those most likely to suffer are the poor, the vulnerable, the powerless.

- Unlimited free markets tend to produce what is in effect an 'option against the poor'.

To what extent are my 'needs' driven by the advertisers?

What steps do I take to protect myself/my family from brain-washing by advertisers' slogans, jingles and images?

The mass media

High standards of broadcasting which are traditional in Britain cannot be taken for granted. The marked decline in standards of broadcasting cannot all be blamed on public taste and demand. Broadcasters play a major part in shaping that taste.

- It is always easier to drive taste downwards than upwards.

Each step is a small one, but the effect is cumulative. Deterioration can happen without any major decision being taken by society.

In the newspaper industry too, the common good is disregarded.

Giving readers 'what they want' is often the only yardstick applied.

There is a need too in journalism to separate the reporting of fact from the presentation of speculation and comment. Journalists and editors need to be aware of their moral responsibility for the good of society.

- It seems to be the case, however, that bad journalism will drive out good.

How critical is my reading of the newspapers?

How might I improve it?

Do I automatically buy the same newspapers, regardless of the standards they subscribe to?

What options have I?

THE WORLD OF WORK

Work is a participation in God's creative activity.

- It increases the common good. Productive action to create wealth is blessed by God and praised by the Church. When respectful of the worker, work can also be a source of fulfilment and satisfaction. It is a right and a duty, and part of God's plan.

- The Church teaches that the rights of workers take precedence over those of capital.

These include the right to decent work, to just wages, to security of employment, to adequate rest and holidays, to safe conditions of work, to non-discrimination, to form and join unions and, as the last resort, to strike.

The Church has always deplored the treatment of employment as nothing more than a form of commercial contract.

- An employed person is a full human being, not a commodity to be bought and sold according to market requirements.

- Employees should be brought into creative partnership with managements.

Profits are a source of a social dividend in which others have a right to benefit.

- Schemes of co-ownership and worker shareholding respect the humanity of the workers.

The Church deplores an 'us' and 'them' divide between managers and workforce and discourages confrontational attitudes in industrial relations.

- The fact of entering into a contract does not of itself guarantee structural justice between a large employer and an isolated individual employee.

> Where in my experience do I detect an 'us' and 'them' divide between managers and workforce, employers and employees?
>
> What can I do about it?

UNIONS

Trade unions have a role in righting such imbalances. The Church upholds a worker's right to membership, in line with the principle of solidarity. Catholic Social Teaching advocates membership of an appropriate union. We note that the decline in union membership in recent years is not necessarily a healthy sign. However, social teaching warns against the dangers of trade unions being too closely associated with political parties.

Employers should not deny workers this right and must be ready to meet union representatives in order to engage in collective bargaining.

Strikes

Unions in turn have a duty to conduct their affairs in accordance with the common good. Before striking, workers must take account of the likely effects of their action on others, whether workers, users or consumers. It is unfair to inflict hardship on third parties as a deliberate tactic. Strikers are in dispute with their employer, not the public.

Wages

Employers have a duty to pay a just wage which takes account of the needs of the individual and not just his or her value on the so-called market.

- It is not morally acceptable to try to reduce unemployment by letting wages fall below the level required to sustain a decent living standard.

Where wages do fall below this level, the State may step in. However, Church teaching does not regard State welfare provision as a desirable substitute for a just wage. Besides, this eventually falls back on the taxpayer.

How do I react when I see imported goods clearly produced in 'sweatshops'?

What are the pros and cons of buying them?

Europe

The Churches have a crucial role to play in safeguarding the moral and spiritual values which gave Europe its soul.

Solidarity and subsidiarity are principles which should also apply to relations between individual states and the wider international community.

Solidarity is expressed in consideration for everyone and everything, from the family right through to the planet. We need to keep the wider perspective.

- It is possible to be both British and European.

The principle of subsidiarity is to be borne in mind in deciding who should make decisions governing social, financial and monetary matters affecting members of the European Union.

Have I thought out the advantages and disadvantages of social, economic and monetary union for the average person, for the small trader, for our responsibilities towards the developing nations?

How might I find out more?

Have I made my views known constructively?

THE GLOBAL COMMON GOOD

In a global society, the term 'common good' must apply worldwide. The principle of solidarity is violated if there are places in the world where basic human needs are not met, or if there are countries too poor to participate in the global economy.

The Catholic Church repeatedly reminds us that an economic order that condemns millions to abject poverty is grossly unjust.

- In recent years solidarity between richer and poorer nations has declined. This trend must be reversed. Overseas aid has a vital part to play in aiding grass-roots development in poorer societies.

The Bishops' Conference of England and Wales has urged successive governments to work towards the United Nations target of allocating 0.7% of the G.N.P. to overseas aid, but without success so far.

How much do I know about the track-record in this regard of the main political parties?

As the election approaches, how could I find out where my local candidates stand on this issue. Could I write to them, or attend one of the pre-election meetings?

In poorer countries, the debt burden perpetuates poverty and halts development at local level.

- We encourage public opinion to support the British government in their efforts to resolve the international debt crisis.

It is dangerous to rely on free market principles alone in economic relations between rich nations and poor. They are unequal partners.

The poorer nations need the protection and co-operation of the rich in their growth towards full participation in the global economy.

Solidarity requires the developed world

- to refrain from promoting arms sales to poor countries;

- to open their markets further to products from those countries;

- to support the setting up of appropriate regional security structures;

- and to refrain from imposing harsh adjustment programmes on the poorest countries, which oblige them to divert resources from health and education with disastrous results, especially for women.

THE ENVIRONMENTAL COMMON GOOD

- Care for the environment is part of caring for the common good.

- To have 'dominion' over the earth does not mean having unlimited freedom to despoil it.

The loving care of nature comes from a deep religious instinct implanted by God.

We are on the earth as gift and privilege and need to cultivate a 'religious respect for the integrity of creation' (The Catechism of the Catholic Church, par. 2415).

- We hold our environmental 'common goods' in trust for future generations; therefore we do not own them outright.

Public authorities in recent years have shown concern for this environmental dimension of the common good. There is need for the creation of effective global authorities to see to it at international level.

What is my reaction when I read or hear of the activities of conservationists and other environmentally aware groups?

OWNERSHIP AND PROPERTY

Ownership is a human right and an ingredient of human freedom, but it is governed by a 'social mortgage' and needs to be restricted.

Greater shareholding is good, but is not automatically enough.

- Investors have a responsibility for the way their shareholdings are used.

Both managers and shareholders have a social responsibility which the law in Britain needs to recognise.

- The economy exists for the human person, not the other way round.

The interests of all 'stakeholders' need to be recognised.

Employers are reminded that employees constitute a reservoir of human effort, wisdom and experience, a form of 'social capital'.

To disregard this is deplorable and a cause of social injustice which is often associated with 'down-sizing' operations.

Do I take the trouble to read and to understand the annual reports sent to me by my bank, my building society, and other companies which use my money?

How much do I know about their investment policies? At home? In the developing countries?

CRISIS IN THE SOCIAL DIMENSION

Party political arguments in Britain over whether or not the 'feel-good' factor is returning have missed the mark. They fail to see that

- the nation's real crisis is not economic, but moral and spiritual.

It is a crisis of individual belief and confusion over personal moral behaviour. But the social dimension is also in crisis, as surveys have shown.

- The British seem to be losing faith in the possibility of a better future.

Increasingly people turn to their private world for personal fulfilment. Human relationships are frequently under pressure as a result.

The British have always had a feeling for 'the common good' even if they have not expressed it in those terms. They are no longer sure that that principle can be ruled upon.

- The common good increasingly appears to be an illusion.

Loss of confidence in this concept is one of the primary factors behind the national mood of pessimism.

The sense of mutual responsibility and the spirit of solidarity are in decline. Even the prospect of the approaching millennium seems to stir no new sense of vision and purpose.

> What can I do to offer hope and a new sense of purpose to young people at this time?
>
> How would I encourage them to harness their generosity and idealism for the good of society as a whole and to put their backs behind the political process?

The principles set out in this document are the necessary minimum conditions for a fair and prosperous society.

A society without those conditions will show many of the symptoms which are present in British society now.

DOMINION OVER THE EARTH

The Second Vatican Council speaks of humanity's sharing in the kingship of Christ. It consists in 'the priority of ethics over technology, in the primacy of the person over things, and the superiority of spirit over matter' (Pope John Paul II, *Redemptor Hominis*, 1979).

- The greatest threats to British society now lie in the growing priority of technology over ethics, of things over persons, of matter over spirit.

- Public life needs rescuing from utilitarian expediency and the pursuit of self-interest.

- Society must not turn its back on poor people nor on the stranger at the gate.

- The twin principles of solidarity and subsidiarity need to be applied systematically to the reform of the institutions of public life.

- The protection of human rights must be reinforced, the mechanisms of democracy repaired, the integrity of the environment defended.

- The common good must be made to prevail, even against strong economic forces that would deny it.

Where in modern society do I see 'the priority of persons over things, etc.' stood on its head?

What examples do I find in today's newspaper? TV news?

What concrete steps might I take to reverse the current trend?

No social trend is beyond reversal.

This is the challenge: to apply Catholic Social Teaching to our society, along with like-minded citizens of every political and religious allegiance.

How do I feel having read this document:
More hopeful?   Why?

Less hopeful?   Why?

The Common Good 47

What passages particularly struck me?

What comments do I wish to record?